Beliefs
Important
to Baptists

Unit II

TEACHER'S EDITION

ROSALIE BECK
DEBORAH McCOLLISTER

BAPTISTWAY®
Dallas, Texas

BAPTISTWAY® Management Team
Executive Director, Baptist General Convention of Texas: Charles Wade
Director, State Missions Commission: James Semple
Director, Bible Study/Discipleship Division: Bernard M. Spooner

Publishing consultant: Ross West, Positive Difference Communications
Cover and Interior Design and Production: Desktop Miracles, Inc.

First edition: October 2000.
ISBN: 1–931060–02–9

Beliefs Important to Baptists: II

Beliefs Important to Baptists

Beliefs Important to Baptists: II contains four lessons on these key beliefs that are important to Baptists:

- Salvation Only by Grace Through Faith
- Soul Competency and the Priesthood of the Believer
- Symbolic Understanding of Baptism and the Lord's Supper
- The Autonomy of the Local Congregation of Believers

These lessons can be used in various settings—such as in an adult Sunday School class, in a Discipleship Training study, in a Wednesday evening study, or in a new member class.

Plan to study all the lessons in *Beliefs Important to Baptists*! (They can be studied in any order.)

Who in the World Are Baptists, Anyway?—A Bible Study Lesson That Summarizes Basic Biblical Understandings About Who Baptists Are, What They Believe, and How They Live

Beliefs Important to Baptists: I

- The Authority of the Bible
- Believer's Baptism and Church Membership
- Congregational Church Government
- Evangelism and Missions

Beliefs Important to Baptists: III

- The Deity and Lordship of Jesus Christ
- The Security of the Believer
- Voluntary Cooperation Among Churches
- Religious Freedom and Separation of Church and State

Beliefs Important to Baptists

Beliefs Important to Baptists is Bible study that is especially related to who the people called Baptists are, what they believe, and how they live. Leading a class in studying the Bible is a sacred trust. This *Teacher's Edition* of *Beliefs Important to Baptists* has been prepared to help you as you give your best to this important task.

Note first that the Bible comments in this *Teacher's Edition* are identical in content to the Bible comments in the member's edition.

Then notice the format of the teaching suggestions. You'll find first a "Teaching Plan." The suggestions in this plan are intended to be practical, helpful, and immediately useful as you prepare to teach. The major headings in the "Teaching Plan" are intended to help you sequence how you teach so as to follow the flow of how people tend to learn. The first major heading, "Connect with Life," provides ideas that will help you begin the class session where your class is and draw your class into the study. The second major heading, "Guide the Study," offers suggestions for helping your class engage the Scriptures actively and develop a greater understanding of this portion of the Bible's message. The third major heading, "Encourage Application," is meant to help participants focus on how to respond with their lives to this message.

In addition to a "Teaching Plan," you'll also find "Additional Teaching Ideas." These ideas may be used as substitutes for or supplements to one or more of the teaching ideas in "Teaching Plan."

Here are ten steps you can take to help you prepare well to teach each lesson and save time in doing so:

1. Prepare your class for this study by providing copies of *Beliefs Important to Baptists* at least a week in advance.

2. Start studying early in the week before your class meets.

3. Consider carefully the suggested main idea and study aim. These can help you discover the main thrust of this particular lesson.

4. Use your Bible to read and consider prayerfully the Scripture passages for the lesson. (The writer has chosen a favorite translation for the lesson. You're free to use the Bible translation you prefer and compare it with the translation chosen, of course.)

5. After reading all the Scripture passages in your Bible, then read the Bible comments in *Beliefs Important to Baptists*. The Bible comments are intended to be an aid to your study of the Bible. Read also the small articles—"sidebars"—in each lesson. They are intended to provide additional, enrichment information and inspiration and to encourage thought and application.

6. Try to answer for yourself the questions included in each lesson. They're intended to encourage further thought and application, and you can also use them in the class session itself.

7. Review "Teaching Plan" and "Additional Teaching Ideas" in this *Teacher's Edition*. Consider how these suggestions would help you teach this Bible passage in your class to accomplish the teaching aim.

8. Consider prayerfully the needs of your class and how to teach so you can help your class learn best.

9. Develop and follow a lesson plan based on the suggestions in this *Teacher's Edition*, with alterations as needed for your class.

10. Enjoy leading your class in discovering the meaning of the Scripture passages and in applying these passages to their lives.

Salvation Only by Grace Through Faith

BACKGROUND SCRIPTURES

Exodus 6:2–8; Matthew 1:21; 4:17; 16:21–26; Luke 1:68–69; 2:28–32; John 1:11–14,29; 3:3–21,36; 5:24; 10:9; Acts 2:21; 4:12; 15:11; 16:25–34; 20:32; Romans 1:16–18; 3:23–25; 4:3–13; 5:8–10; 10:9–13; Galatians 2:20; 3:13; 6:15; Ephesians 1:7; 2:8–22; Hebrews 5:8–9; 9:24–28; 1 John 2:1–2; Revelation 3:20

FOCAL TEXTS

Acts 16:25–34; Romans 1:16–18; Galatians 2:20; Ephesians 2:8–10

MAIN IDEA

"Salvation by grace means salvation as a free gift on God's part. . . . Receiving salvation as an unmerited gift on God's part is faith."[1]

STUDY AIM

To explain the way of salvation

QUICK READ

Two facets of God's grace are the grace of salvation and the grace of daily living. God saves us, not just from hell, but *to* a specific lifestyle.

Sunday as I looked at the folks in my Sunday School class, my fellow choir members, and the congregation of friends, I understood God's grace in a new way. Yes, God saves us from sin and hell, but God also saves us to be the Lord's children, part of the community of faith. Salvation is by grace through faith; we cannot earn salvation or membership in the body of believers. God's grace, the "unearned merit," reaches into our lives, establishes an eternal, life-saving relationship between ourselves and God, and grafts us into the body of Christ. We thus are God's children in a family, not orphans left alone to make our way through the world. God performs this miracle in our lives without coercion of any type. The Lord requires only our faith.

Midnight Salvation (Acts 16:25–34)

As a child, I liked the story of the Philippian jailer (Acts 16:25–34). As an adult, I marvel at the powerful way God saved the jailer and affirmed the work of Paul and Silas. What a scene! Midnight, a stinking jail cell, stinging whip marks, and two men singing!

The Philippian officials jailed Paul and Silas because of false accusations, beat them without a hearing, and consigned them to the care of the jailer (see 16:16–24). The jailer understood these men needed special guarding. So he placed them in the most interior, lightless, and well-guarded cell in the prison. Chained to stocks, Paul and Silas had no way to escape. The jailer made sure these prisoners were secure because if they escaped he would be executed in their stead. This is the scene from which God's grace would pour into the lives of the jailer and his household.

In the face of possible death, Paul and Silas sang and prayed. At a time when I would have curled up in the fetal position and withdrawn, these two missionaries continued in strong fellowship with God. What faith! Both had experienced the grace of God. God had saved Paul, a persecutor and hater of the church, in a spectacular manner on the road to Damascus (9:1–30). Silas was a leader of the Jerusalem church (15:22).

Acts 16:25–34[2]

[25]About midnight Paul and Silas were praying and singing hymns to God, and the prisoners were listening to them. [26]Suddenly there was an earthquake, so violent that the foundations of the prison were shaken; and immediately all the doors were opened and everyone's chains were unfastened. [27]When the jailer woke up and saw the prison doors wide open, he drew his sword and was about to kill himself, since he supposed that the prisoners had escaped. [28]But Paul shouted in a loud voice, "Do not harm yourself, for we are all here." [29]The jailer called for lights, and rushing in, he fell down trembling before Paul and Silas. [30]Then he brought them outside and said, "Sirs, what must I do to be saved?" [31]They answered, "Believe on the Lord Jesus, and you will be saved, you and your household." [32]They spoke the word of the Lord to him and to all who were in his house. [33]At the same hour of the night he took them and washed their wounds; then he and his entire family were baptized without delay. [34]He brought them up into the house and set food before them; and he and his entire household rejoiced that he had become a believer in God.

Romans 1:16–18

[16]For I am not ashamed of the gospel; it is the power of God for salvation to everyone who has faith, to the Jew first and also to the Greek. [17]For in it the righteousness of God is revealed through faith for faith; as it is written, "The one who is righteous will live by faith."

[18]For the wrath of God is revealed from heaven against all ungodliness and wickedness of those who by their wickedness suppress the truth.

Galatians 2:20

. . . It is no longer I who live, but it is Christ who lives in me. And the life I now live in the flesh I live by faith in the Son of God, who loved me and gave himself for me.

Although in pain and facing an uncertain future, Paul and Silas knew God worked in every trial. Thus they responded with hymns and prayer. Perhaps they sang the first-century equivalent of "Amazing Grace" and prayed that God's will be done. In the face of adversity, God's grace enabled them to live in the moment and to believe God's presence would sustain them. Supporting each other, they presented Christ to their fellow inmates.

The jailer finished his duties and went to bed, leaving the prisoners to their fears and dark thoughts. But as Paul and Silas prayed, sang, and witnessed for the Lord, the felons surrounding them listened. I have a mental image of prisoners straining against cell bars to hear more clearly what these two men said and sang. Through the murk of the prison came sounds of hope, peace, and promise—sounds the felons hadn't heard for many years or perhaps had never heard. The faithfulness of Paul and Silas communicated hope to the hopeless in that dank place.

How do you and I react in times of uncertainty and pain? Do we go to God or withdraw from God?

God's love and grace don't depend on our circumstances. They are constant in our lives. The *Baptist Faith and Message* of 1963 uses the terms "regeneration," "sanctification," and "glorification" to explain the process of salvation (Article 4). As stated in an old adage, we have been saved from the punishment of sin (regeneration), we are being saved from the power of sin (sanctification), and we will be saved from the presence of

Ephesians 2:8–10

[8]For by grace you have been saved through faith, and this is not your own doing; it is the gift of God—[9]not the result of works, so that no one may boast. [10]For we are what he has made us, created in Christ Jesus for good works, which God prepared beforehand to be our way of life.

sin (glorification). God implants saving grace in our souls when we become believers. How we respond to that grace in times of trial says more about us than about God. Paul and Silas responded with faith and courage.

God sometimes uses spectacular means to get our attention. In the case of the Philippian jailer, an earthquake hit the jail to grab his attention. At midnight, when the jailer slept soundly and God's followers sang hymns, an earthquake shook the chains from the prisoners, swung open cell doors, and freed the felons. Awakened, the jailer ran to check his wards. He assumed they had fled the prison. Losing prisoners, especially two such important ones as Paul and Silas, would have meant the jailer's death. Rather than face public execution, he decided to commit suicide. Before he could, Paul called to him. A word of salvation, of hope, came out of the darkness. What an unexpected reprieve from death!

The jailer immediately wanted what made these two men different, what gave them the courage to sing, to pray, and to stay when they had the chance to flee. Quietly and simply, Paul told the jailer, "'Believe on the Lord Jesus'" (16:31). Paul created no requirements before salvation. He did not require the jailer to stop sacrificing to idols before salvation, and he did not question the jailer about his political or moral views on critical issues of the day before extending God's grace. The only act on the jailer's part in the process of salvation was to believe in the Lord Jesus. So simple but so profound.

Paul also made a promise to the jailer (see 16:31). If you believe, your household will be influenced, too. Community comes with belief. A life-changing event affects those close to the person saved, and God's grace flows through believers into the aching hearts of the lost. Without hesitation, the jailer accepted God's grace and took Paul and Silas to his home for medical attention. While there, the two men continued their task of witnessing, and the jailer's household came to the Lord. From the grace of God and the faithfulness of two prisoners, a new community of faith emerged.

"'Believe on the Lord Jesus, and you will be saved, you and your household'" (16:31). Such a plain, straightforward way of introducing someone to God. No frills, no barriers, just faith.

What barriers do we put in the way of people seeking the Lord? What barriers do we place in our own path as we seek to follow Christ? One thing we can know with certainty—God's grace surmounts and destroys all barriers.

A Tower Experience (Romans 1:16–18)

Martin Luther (1483–1546) found no peace, no matter how many hours he spent in confession, no matter how much he beat himself, no matter how strongly he longed for relationship with God. Even as a monk and a priest, peace eluded Luther's grasp. He yearned for acceptance by God. One day, as he sat in a tower room preparing a seminary lecture on Romans 1:16–18, the gospel smacked him right between the eyes. God transferred Luther's focus from the wrath of God consuming all sinners to God's grace saving through faith.

The Protestant Reformation latched onto this insight, and as Baptists developed in the early 1600s, they affirmed Luther's emphasis that salvation is *sola gratias*—solely of grace. We don't gain salvation by being baptized as infants or by being born in America. We don't earn salvation by growing up in a Baptist church or by going to a Baptist school. The true gospel "is the power of God for salvation to everyone who has faith . . . " (Romans 1:16). Salvation comes by the Lord's grace to those who believe.

In our age of tolerance, we easily forget that people need God's grace. Romans 1:18 reminds us that God's wrath is real. People need to know that eternal consequences flow from their actions and attitudes. We ignore opportunities to share the gospel because we don't want to be labeled as fanatics. We remain silent in the face of

Lottie Moon

Lottie Moon lived the gospel daily. Although she made mistakes like all of us, she modeled Christ's love to the Chinese with whom she worked. Adopting their dress, eating their food, and mastering their language, she became a "little Christ" for the people of Ping Tu for several decades. God's grace poured into folks in Ping Tu because Lottie Moon accepted God's power to live a Christian life, and because they responded in faith to the gospel. Illness plagued her. Fatigue made her feel inadequate for the task. The lack of trained missionary personnel made her work overwhelming. Yet, in it all, she persevered in sharing the gospel by word and deed.

Unable to address men directly because of cultural norms, when she spoke to women inside a house, she raised her voice and articulated each word so that the men gathered outside near the windows heard the gospel clearly. From baking cookies for the town's children, to offering aid to the poor and spiritual guidance to new Christians, Charlotte Diggs Moon lived the gospel, a life of good works.

immorality or sin because we don't want to appear judgmental. We cling to the gift of God's grace for ourselves, hope others find it, too, and yet do little to share that word of grace. How sad. Luther's insight caused him to explode into his religious world with the radical claim that God's grace is sufficient. What will our insight into God's grace cause us to do?

God reminds us of Paul and Silas in prison, and God will grant us the courage to explain the gospel to a person in spiritual need. As we live in God's grace, the Lord guides us to take loving stands on important moral issues in our world. By ones and twos, by families and congregations, we can make a difference in the spiritual and moral lives of those around us. As members of the body of Christ, we gain strength to accomplish godly purposes, and wisdom to live as Christians. But we must be willing to share God's simple message—"'Believe on the Lord Jesus'" (Acts 16:31).

God's Grace in Daily Life
(Galatians 2:20; Ephesians 2:8–10)

From the early 1600s when Baptists began writing confessions of faith to let the world know what a particular community of faith believed, Baptists have asserted that salvation comes by grace through faith. This idea shaped the Baptist understanding of baptism, the Lord's Supper, the function of the church, and the need to share the gospel. Salvation by grace defines who we are as Baptists.

God lays claim to our lives. In Galatians 2:20, Paul explained the place of the Lord's grace in our lives: ". . . it is no longer I who live, but it is Christ who lives in me. And the life I now live in the flesh I live by faith in the Son of God, who loved me and gave himself for me." If we take this doctrine seriously, we should live our lives as "little Christs" wherever we are. "Christ in us" means we share our knowledge of God's gift of salvation with a world that desperately needs that knowledge. We cannot create faith, and we cannot create grace. We can, however, create an understanding of God's desire for relationship with those we know, and we can live out God's grace in our world. The Baptist doctrine of salvation by grace through faith means we share the gospel each moment by how we live, how we present "Christ in us." Let us live a deliberate, consistent, and grace-filled gospel before the world.

God's gracious gift of salvation is free, but it is also costly! Christ demands our all. As we come to the Lord, we live daily in faith. Too, as God's grace embraces our lives, we embrace our world with faith, love, and grace. In a real sense, we are pathways for God's grace into the world. We extend God's promises to people who need those promises. Christ

Living a "Christ" Life

1. Set aside a time each day to spend at least ten minutes in prayer.
2. Ask God to guide each decision you make, each word you speak, and each gesture you make during the day.
3. Be silent for five minutes, allowing God time to speak to you.
4. As you face tough situations during the day, silently ask for God's grace to surround the issue.
5. Before going to bed, thank God for evidence of God's grace during the day.

lives in us to sustain us and through us to sustain the world. What a wonderful way to experience God!

In Ephesians 2:8–10, Paul reminds us that salvation is God's grace-gift. Verse 10 also reminds us that this gift lays claim to our lives. God calls us to live godly lives. Salvation, as we already have noted, is a process that includes regeneration (saved), sanctification (being saved), and glorification (will be saved). The words in parentheses in the previous sentence refer to what we might call the "tenses" of the Christian life. Regeneration speaks of *having been saved*, sanctification of *being saved*, and glorification of *will be saved*, referring to the fullness of salvation that is yet to come. Walking with God daily is as much a grace-gift part of salvation as being saved from eternal damnation. In some ways, we find it more difficult to live a godly life than to accept Christ by faith. Sharing our faith and living as God would have us to live come as part of the process, however. Do we take the "daily" part of salvation seriously enough?

Baptists take the gospel very seriously. As stated by Paul in Romans 1:18, the unworthy will fall under God's wrath, and we believe all humans fit that description. Without Christ, no one can be a child of God or accept God's grace. We support missions and evangelism to bring the knowledge of Christ to the world. Yet, we find it easier to give money to missions or to pay a preacher than to live a Christian life that presents the gospel to the world, in word and deed.

"For we are what he [God] has made us, created in Christ Jesus for good works, which God prepared beforehand to be our way of life" (Eph. 2:10). "Our way of life" is to do "good works." What a challenge! Being Christ in the world is a difficult task. But Paul assured us, from his life story and from his writing, that God's grace proves sufficient for our daily lives. When was the last time we began our days with a "thank you" for the grace to get through the next twenty-four hours as a "little Christ" in the world? How often do we experience God's power in daily life? What effort do we put forth to live out our faith in God's grace through our personal relationships, within our families, and in our work habits?

Paul promised us, and as Baptists we take this promise seriously, that God intends us to walk with the Lord each moment. Stumbling over spiritual obstacles, erecting ungodly barriers, we forget that the Lord knows what we face and provides more than enough grace to meet our needs.

God made us for good works, to be "little Christs" in the world, and told us exactly what doing good works means. (See Romans 12:1–2, for example.) We need to participate deliberately in God's plan each day. Saved from the punishment of sin, we must live saved from the power of sin, and we will be saved from the presence of sin. The gospel is the message we are to share with the world.

Too, we are to live our daily lives as members of a community of faith, accountable to one another and to God for our attitudes, beliefs, and lives. By accepting wise counsel, godly advice, and loving inspiration, we benefit from God's grace. The promise of salvation includes membership in a church family. God provides a community of believers to provide encouragement, to help us make tough decisions, and to enable us to work through grief and distress. We struggle side-by-side with other Christians, learning how to be God's children and how to share that knowledge with the world. As Baptists, we believe that God's grace empowers us to live Christ-like lives, supported by a community of faith. Praise God, from whom all blessings flow!

QUESTIONS

1. When did you last share the gospel verbally? How did it feel?

2. Within you, what barriers exist to sharing the gospel with co-workers or family?

3. How might God overcome those barriers?

4. Looking at the last year, what experiences of God's grace can you point to?

5. Who in your church shared God's grace with you?

6. With whom have you shared God's grace?

Notes

1. Walter Thomas Conner, *Christian Doctrine* (Nashville, Tennessee: Broadman Press, 1937), 197.
2. Unless otherwise indicated, all Scripture quotes are from the New Revised Standard Version.

Salvation Only by Grace Through Faith

TEACHING AIM

To help the class explain the way of salvation

TEACHING PLAN

Connect with Life

1. Write on the board: "Fear!" Comment that all human beings fear something, such as heights or darkness. Ask the class to help you list on the board some other things people are afraid of.

2. Point out that some fears even relate to the spiritual life, such as these: whether God will love us or save us if we are sinful; whether we have done all the right things—dotted all the *I*s and crossed all the *T*s—in order to be assured of salvation. Suggest that today's lesson will remind us of the way to salvation.

Guide the Study

3. Referring to Acts 16:22–24, point out that Paul and Silas had reason to be despondent. They had been ridiculed, beaten severely, and thrown into the innermost part of a prison. Encourage your class to imagine what they must have heard there, how the place must have smelled in the midst of such human suffering, and how they must have felt physically.

4. Invite the class to read Acts 16:25 silently to see how Paul and Silas behaved under these circumstances. Refer to these thoughts from the lesson comments under "Midnight Salvation (Acts 16:25–34)":

   . . . We have been saved from the punishment of sin (regeneration), we are being saved from the power of sin (sanctification), and we will be saved from the presence of sin (glorification). God implants saving grace in our souls when we become believers. How we respond to that grace in times of trial says more about us than about God. Paul and Silas responded with faith and courage.

5. Write on the board these points that refer to the Philippian jailer:
   • The greatest crisis of his life
   • The greatest question of his life
   • The greatest gift of his life

   Ask someone to read Acts 16:26–34 aloud. Ask the class to listen for how these bulleted points summarize these verses. Invite responses to each point.

6. Now focus on verse 31. Ask, What was required for the jailer's salvation? (belief in the Lord Jesus) Then ask the class to list ideas about what was *not* required. Examples of responses include these: baptism (which is a result of, not a condition for salvation); good works (The jailer's kindness was a result, not a condition, of salvation.); giving money; having great knowledge of Scripture; having a certain moral stance on an issue.

7. Share this quotation from Dr. Bill Pinson, Executive Director Emeritus of the Executive Board of the Baptist General Convention of Texas: "Thus Baptists declare it is this unique grace/faith that brings salvation—nothing else . . . not grace/faith plus church membership, or plus baptism, or plus good works, or plus sacrament but grace/faith plus nothing."[1]

8. Ask, Who can receive salvation? Invite members to read aloud with you Romans 1:16–18 in order to answer the question. Use the Scripture from the lesson comments so all will read from the same translation. Receive responses after the reading. Point out that

although it is clear that everyone who believes receives salvation (verse 16) and is made righteous by faith (verse 17), verse 18 clarifies that with God it is *not* "anything goes!" God's wrath is real, but all may receive God's grace through belief in Christ.

9. Remind the class that the concept of grace is not limited to something we received in the past. As the lesson comments state, "The Baptist doctrine of salvation by grace through faith means we share the gospel each moment by how we live, how we present 'Christ in us.'" With that thought in mind, have someone read aloud Galatians 2:20. Note that we are extensions of Christ—of God's grace—in the world.

10. Note that a favorite Scripture among Baptist believers is Ephesians 2:8–10, and ask the class to read these verses silently. Note that the Greek verb for "saved" in verse 8 implies a process but suggests that the process is completed and existing in a finished state. The meaning thus is that we *have been saved*. In other New Testament passages, it is established that we are *being saved* (see 1 Corinthians 1:18), and that we *will be saved* (see Romans 13:11; Hebrews 9:27–28).

11. Ask the class to consider the implications of living in this grace process—living out grace in our daily lives. Grace saved us, and grace continuously saves us. What attitudes should we thus show in how we live?

Encourage Application

12. Circle back to the fear issue mentioned at the beginning of the lesson by asking, How can an understanding of salvation through grace affect our fears? our attitudes towards others' need to be saved? our pride? other areas of our lives?

13. Set aside several minutes for guided meditation and prayer at the end of the session, asking members to close their eyes and converse with God about these issues:
   • Have I believed in the Lord Jesus in order to be saved?
   • How has God shown his grace towards me in the past?

- How will grace save me when this life is over?
- During the coming week, how might God's grace in my life be evident?

ADDITIONAL TEACHING IDEAS

Connect with Life: *Case Studies*. Read these case studies and invite responses:

A. Jessica, a teenager, has come to you after hearing a sermon. The sermon implied that if she had not followed a certain process step by step, had not prayed a certain prayer, or had not done certain things since the time she thought she was saved, she probably was not saved. Although Jessica had thought she was saved at a young age and had made a profession of faith, she is now wondering whether she did the right things to be saved. What would you say to her?

B. You work with a very moral, upstanding person. Everyone knows that Sam is kind, that he loves his family, and that he is sincere in all his moral views. One day Sam comments that he believes that since God loves everybody, one sincere religion is as good as another. How would you respond to his comment?

Guide the Study: *Scripture Reflection*. Invite someone to read aloud Romans 12:1–3. Based upon these Scripture verses, ask members to name the ways in which grace should affect our daily lives. List their responses on the board.

Encourage Application: *Hymn Reflection*. Ask members to read all the stanzas of "Amazing Grace" from a hymnal. After each stanza is read, ask the class to reflect on how it reflects the biblical truths discussed today. Inquire, Which of the stanzas seem to be most relevant in your life right now?

Notes

1. William M. Pinson, Jr., Sermon, "The Baptist Way," 1996. (Provided by the Baptist Distinctives Committee of the Baptist General Convention of Texas, Dallas, Texas.)

Soul Competency and the Priesthood of the Believer

BACKGROUND SCRIPTURES

Genesis 1:26–27; 2:7; Exodus 19:1–6; Psalm 8; 42:1–2;
Jeremiah 31:29–34; Ezekiel 18:1–4; Matthew 16:13–17;
John 3:1–16; 8:36; 14:12; Acts 4:12; 1 Corinthians 3:21,23;
Galatians 5:1,13; Ephesians 2:11–21; Hebrews 4:14–16; 8:8–13;
1 Peter 2:4–10; Revelation 5:1–10

FOCAL TEXTS

Genesis 1:26–27; Jeremiah 31:29–34; Matthew 16:16–17;
John 3:16; 1 Peter 2:4–10

MAIN IDEA

"There should be no institution, human person, rite, or system which stands between the individual person and God. . . . All have equal access to the Father's table, the Father's ear, and the Father's heart."[1]

STUDY AIM

To identify implications of soul competency and the priesthood of the believer

QUICK READ

Baptists believe in the priesthood of the believer and the soul competency of a believer. We believe we relate to God without human mediators, both as individuals and as a body of believers.

Religious freedom is a precious liberty. Baptists have battled legislatures, congresses, local authorities, and each other for the right of all people to worship, or not worship, God in their own way. The demand for religious liberty comes from the Baptist doctrines of soul competency and the priesthood of a believer or believers.

From Thomas Helwys to Roger Williams to George Truett, mainstream Baptist leaders have contended that each person bears responsibility for his or her relationship with God. An individual has the God-given competency to respond to God or not. An individual has the right and responsibility to interpret Scripture and apply biblical teachings to life. No authority has the power to coerce belief.

For generations Baptist laypeople and theologians, ministers and Sunday School teachers, have asserted these twin doctrines of right and responsibility. Some folks have even died to make the point that God gives every woman and man the competency to encounter the Lord, and that each believer has the responsibility to act as a priest before the Lord.

In the Beginning . . . (Genesis 1:26–27)

During the sixth creative event, according to Genesis 1:26–27, God made humans in the divine image. Then God gave the females and males "dominion" over everything else. What a sweeping statement and great responsibility!

Each time I teach Hebrew Bible to college freshmen, I ask the question, "How are we in God's image?" Sometimes they respond that we look like God, but I remind them that God is Spirit, and that the Hebrews condemned images and forbade making idols. With a bit of prompting, the students come up with some ways we reflect God's being. Consider these:

- Humans are rational beings. We can think, identify our emotions, make decisions, and accept responsibility.
- Women and men are religious beings. No matter what civilization

Genesis 1:26–27

26Then God said, "Let us make humankind in our image, according to our likeness; and let them have dominion over the fish of the sea, and over the birds of the air, and over the cattle, and over all the wild animals of the earth, and over every creeping thing that creeps upon the earth." 27 So God created humankind in his image,
in the image of God he created them;
male and female he created them.

Jeremiah 31:29–34

29 In those days they shall no longer say:
"The parents have eaten sour grapes,
and the children's teeth are set on edge."
30But all shall die for their own sins; the teeth of everyone who eats sour grapes shall be set on edge.
31The days are surely coming, says the LORD, when I will make a new covenant with the house of Israel and the house of Judah. 32It will not be like the covenant that I made with their ancestors when I took them by the hand to bring them out of the land of Egypt—a covenant that they broke, though I was their husband, says the LORD. 33But this is the covenant that I will make with the house of Israel after those days, says the LORD: I will put my law within them, and I will write it on their hearts; and I will be their God, and they shall be my people. 34No longer shall they teach one another, or say to each other, "Know the LORD," for they shall all know me, from the least of them to the greatest, says the LORD; for I will forgive their iniquity, and remember their sin no more.

Matthew 16:16–17

16Simon Peter answered, "You are the Messiah, the Son of the living God." 17And Jesus answered him, "Blessed are you, Simon son of Jonah! For flesh and blood has not revealed this to you, but my Father in heaven.

John 3:16

"For God so loved the world that he gave his only Son, so that every-one who believes in him may not perish but may have eternal life."

1 Peter 2:4–10

[4]Come to him, a living stone, though rejected by mortals yet chosen and precious in God's sight, and [5]like living stones, let yourselves be built into a spiritual house, to be a holy priesthood, to offer spiritual sacrifices acceptable to God through Jesus Christ. [6]For it stands in scripture:

"See, I am laying in Zion a stone,

a cornerstone chosen and precious;

and whoever believes in him will not be put to shame."

[7]To you then who believe, he is precious; but for those who do not believe,

"The stone that the builders rejected

has become the very head of the corner,"

[8]and

"A stone that makes them stumble,

and a rock that makes them fall."

They stumble because they disobey the word, as they were destined to do.

[9]But you are a chosen race, a royal priesthood, a holy nation, God's own people, in order that you may proclaim the mighty acts of him who called you out of darkness into his marvelous light.

[10] Once you were not a people,

but now you are God's people;

once you had not received mercy,

but now you have received mercy.

an anthropologist finds or an archeologist digs up, that people group has a religion of some sort. They practice a religion.

- People are moral beings, recognizing good and evil. Cultures define "good" and "evil" differently, but all people have moral "slots" in their minds. Created in God's image, we think, make decisions, have religious yearnings, and have a sense of morality.

God gave us the capacity to make religious decisions, to recognize God's handiwork. God made us accountable for these abilities. God gave us soul competency because the Lord wanted uncoerced relationships to grow between ourselves and God.

Jesus modeled this doctrine for us. At no time in his ministry did he resort to force to make a point or coercion to create a positive response. In fact, when the disciples wanted to destroy an unfriendly village (Luke 9:51–56) and Peter cut off Malchus's ear (Matthew 26:47–55; John 18:10), Jesus rebuked the use of force to gain any spiritual end. True belief shines when people exercise their soul competency, when they use their God-given capacity to choose to follow God, not when someone suffers punishment if they don't conform religiously to a norm set by an authority. We have soul competency. God made us in the divine image, making us responsible for our decisions about relating to the Lord. No one can force true belief.

God Made a Promise . . . (Jeremiah 31:29–34)

The children of Israel lived with despair after the Babylonians took them into Exile and destroyed Jerusalem and the temple in 587 BC. Demoralized by their plight, the Hebrews asked tough questions. Has God deserted us? Can we worship God in this foreign place? Why did this happen?

God raised up prophets to help the Israelites answer these questions. One such prophet was Jeremiah of Anathoth. Jeremiah worked for more than forty years as a prophet in Judah. From the time of good King Josiah, through three Babylonian invasions, through an assassination attempt, Jeremiah wrestled with these questions. Through his writings, Jeremiah helped the Hebrews in Babylonia deal with their new life, and he affirmed God's presence with and care for the exiles. He affirmed that God had not deserted them, that they could worship God in Babylonia without the temple, and that their sin caused the destruction of Judah.

God gave Jeremiah a new insight into the way God wanted to relate to people. In Jeremiah 31:29–34, the prophet presented the New Covenant. Unlike the Mosaic Covenant, which the Law fleshed out for daily life and which focused on the creation of a Hebrew political state, the New Covenant emphasized the individual nature of religious commitment to God.

Thomas Helwys

In the early 1600s Thomas Helwys wrote a pamphlet titled *The Mystery of Iniquity*. In it he called for complete religious freedom in Great Britain. He presented a simple argument. Each person will stand before God and be judged alone. So, each individual must have the freedom to make spiritual decisions without coercion, because they will be judged for their choices. King James I sent Helwys to jail. The Baptist preacher died there.

What was most important to Helwys was not that he wrote the first plea for complete religious freedom published in England or that he served as pastor of the first Baptist church on English soil. What was most important to Helwys was that each person must relate to God individually in choosing to be a Christian, interpreting Scripture, and living a godly life under the direction of the Holy Spirit. Helwys paid dearly for his affirmation of the Baptist doctrine of soul competency and the priesthood of believers, but he considered it a price worth paying.

In verses 29–30, Jeremiah took the exiles to task for blaming their ancestors for their suffering. In traditional Hebrew life, the decisions of the head of the tribe affected all people in the clan. This corporate identity shifted with Jeremiah's firm insistence that each person is accountable to God for his or her own life. Community responsibility remained strong for the Hebrews, but spiritual life begins within the individual's decision regarding God. A parent can not choose God for a child, and neither can a child choose God for a parent. Each person, exercising soul competency, must choose or reject God by his or her own will.

With the New Covenant, God makes no promise regarding the creation of a political state. Rather, the promise concerns the spiritual state of each person. The Lord will inscribe the divine law on the hearts of believers, and they will know God. External sources can help clarify, explain, and teach, but it is in the personal relationship that God comes to a believer. Jeremiah does not minimize the importance of external influences in helping chart a person's spiritual growth. Rather the prophet stresses that the ultimate relationship is between God and the heart of a believer whose soul is competent to choose the Lord.

Fulfilled by Jesus . . . (Matthew 16:16–17; John 3:16)

Every major religion has priests. No matter what the religion, a priest has two functions: to lead in worship and to mediate between God and the world. The priest takes the world's needs to God and brings God's word to the world. Priests may function somewhat differently from religion to religion, but priests hold a special place in all religions.

Baptists teach that believers are priests. Each one has the responsibility to relate to God, to understand the Bible, and to interact with the Holy Spirit. We teach that God reveals God's self to each believer and that a Christian has the responsibility to respond to God's direction.

Matthew 16:16–17 illustrates this belief. Jesus withdrew from Jewish territory to rest and teach his closest followers on several occasions. One time they went to the resort town of Caesarea Philippi on a retreat, and Jesus posed the question (Matt. 16:13), "'Who do people say that the Son of Man is?'" After several different responses came from the disciples, Jesus asked, "'But who do you say that I am?'" Peter, the irrepressible, impetuous fisherman, blurted out, "You are the Messiah, the Son of the living God" (16:16).

I have heard many sermons on what Peter meant when he made that statement and on his faulty understanding of "messiah." Whatever Peter meant, Jesus complimented his statement by noting that God gave that insight to the fisherman. This text teaches many important truths about Jesus, messiahship, redemption, and courage. But it also underscores the Baptist doctrine of the priesthood of a believer. God dealt with Peter directly. The Lord did not go through a mediating human but went straight to the heart of the disciple and implanted truth.

We don't depend on mediators to bring God to us, because God comes to each of us in God's time and God's way. The Lord does use other believers to teach, heal, guide, and help us along our spiritual pathway. Our salvation, however, is not dependent on the actions of another human being. Our salvation depends only on God and our response to God. We are priests before the Lord, relating to God directly.

As a Journeyman missionary in Vietnam in 1973–1975, the first Scripture verse I memorized in Vietnamese was John 3:16. Years earlier I had learned it as a GA, and I had sung it in church choirs. But somehow, when I spoke the verse in Vietnamese, new meaning sprang from the text and imbedded itself in my heart.

An incredibly simple statement of the gospel, John 3:16 says it all. God did it; God did it perfectly; God did it with love; now, the responsibility rests with people to decide their response. This verse does not set up an elaborate hierarchy to mediate salvation or truth to the world. This verse states that the mediation is between Christ and the individual who believes. No middle-person comes on the scene. God sets a very simple criterion for salvation: belief. And we must decide what to do. We must go to God as believers and accept what God offers, depending only on God's promise fulfilled in the incarnation. If God keeps God's promises, we need no other mediator to be saved.

We Are Now God's Priests (1 Peter 2:4–10)

One of the things I do that brings me the most fun is to show students the beautiful ties between the Old and New Testaments, and how the early church picked up on so many of God's promises made before the time of Jesus. First Peter 2:4–10 models the marvelous continuity of Scripture. The passage also affirms an important variation of the Baptist doctrine of the priesthood of the believer.

The First Letter of Peter offered encouragement to Christians who suffered persecution for their faith. Ridiculed as idiots, immoral people, and troublemakers, the early believers suffered greatly at the hands of local officials as well as the Roman Empire. The letter gave comfort and encouragement to the hurting church members by rehearsing some of their religious history, and by showing how Jesus fulfilled prophecy they took very seriously. By drawing on the Old Testament, the letter gave validity to the church's claims that Jesus was Messiah, God in human form.

Case Study

You teach a Bible study class at your church. One of the members, a serious young Christian, has studied 1 Corinthians 11:5 and decided that the women of the church should wear head coverings. Given the doctrines of soul competency and the priesthood of believers, how would you deal with this situation? What would you say or suggest?

Verses 4–8 bring up familiar images: a stone rejected by a builder becoming a cornerstone and Christians as living stones being built into God's temple. These verses echo Paul's teaching in Ephesians 2:21–22. They also recite the Old Testament prophecies in Psalm 118:22; Isaiah 8:14; 28:16. God constructs the church from the individual building blocks of believers' lives. For persecuted believers, these words brought peace and hope, encouragement and comfort.

I always get excited when I have a chance to write or preach on 1 Peter 2:9–10, because these verses tie so wonderfully to God's promises from the Old Testament. In Exodus 19:5–6, God laid out the basic elements of the Mosaic Covenant for the Hebrew people. God made three promises to the Hebrews if they would obey the word of the Lord. If a Hebrew would keep God's commandments to show her or his love for the Lord, in return God would show divine love by keeping the three promises—to make of the Hebrew people a special treasure, a royal priesthood, and a holy nation.

Although we will focus on the "royal priesthood" promise, let's look quickly at the other two promises mentioned in both 1 Peter 2:9 and Exodus 19:5–6. God's chosen people, God's special treasure, alludes to a fact of ancient oriental life. A ruler owned everything in the realm—air, land, people, commerce. The ruler held it all for the next generation's use. The ruler, however, would have a "special treasure" that belonged to the monarch alone. The ruler could do with this "special treasure" whatever he or she wanted. Similarly, God created everything and owned all that existed, but the Hebrews constituted God's "special treasure."

God also promised to make the Hebrews a "holy nation" (1 Pet. 2:9; Ex. 19:5). To that end, God gave the Law so the Hebrews would know how to live. Being "holy" meant living a separated, pure life devoted to good. The rules found in the Old Testament provided guidelines for how to be a holy nation, how to separate themselves from their unbelieving neighbors. First Peter draws this theme from Exodus 19 and claims the church is God's holy nation now. Set apart by lifestyle and a desire for goodness and wholeness, believers live within God's commands given through the life and teaching of Jesus. To love God with everything and to love others as ourselves (Matthew 22:34–40)—these characteristics should define the "holy nation" of the church.

God promised in 1 Peter 2:9 (see Ex. 19:6) to make believers a "royal priesthood." For Baptists, the Lord fulfilled this promise by creating a community of faith. The church is the "new Israel" (see Galatians 6:16). Our doctrine affirms that as a community of faith we learn from each other, pray for each other, and mediate God to the world.

First Peter 2:9–10 teaches that the Christ-event fulfilled God's promise by making the church a priesthood of believer*s*. Note the plural—*believers*. We are not lone rangers, on our own in the big, bad world. We are a people who have both individually and corporately related to God as priests. Thus, the body of Christ, through the priesthood of believers, mediates the world to God and God to the world. As good Baptists, we talk about this act with words like "evangelism" and "missions" rather than "mediation." But the intent is the same. By mediating God to the world, we seek to bring people to a point of exercising their soul competency to choose Christ. We also seek to mediate the needs of the world to God through prayer and responsible citizenship.

Are the concepts of priesthood of the believer and priesthood of the believer*s* in conflict? No! One complements the other. As cooperating Baptists, we mediate God to the world through evangelism and missions, but as individual believers, we stand responsible before the Lord for our individual lives and actions in the church, in the home, and in the workplace. We mediate God to the world through how we live our lives and how we witness to the Lord. First Peter 2:4–10 contends that we are individuals responsible to and relating to God, but we also form a body of believers with responsibilities before the Lord. The two forms of priesthood complement one another, strengthen each other, and support the basic Baptist and Christian belief that God saves.

QUESTIONS

1. How does the priesthood of the believer work out in your life?

2. Does anyone, according to this Baptist doctrine, have the right to tell you what to believe or how to interpret the Bible?

3. How does your church function as a priesthood of believers?

4. What are some implications of the doctrine of soul competency for American politics?

Notes

1. Herschel H. Hobbs and E.Y. Mullins, *The Axioms of Religion*, rev. ed. (Nashville, Tennessee: Broadman Press, 1978), 75.

Soul Competency and the Priesthood of the Believer

TEACHING AIM

To lead the class to identify implications of soul competency and the priesthood of the believer

TEACHING PLAN

Connect with Life

1. Share this story: The story is told that when Chief Justice Charles Evans Hughes walked the aisle to become a member of Calvary Baptist Church in Washington, D.C., a Chinese laundry man came forward at the same time. In receiving them both into membership, the pastor commented that the ground is level at the foot of the cross.[1]

2. Point out that Baptists have long cherished the *right* of every person to approach God directly, without a human mediator. Note that we have taught also the corresponding *responsibility* of every Christian. Suggest that today we will examine this belief—soul competency and the priesthood of the believer—based on the Scriptures.

Guide the Study

3. Before class, collect about four pictures of several people of different ages and backgrounds—such as an adorable baby, someone who looks "down and out," a person at church or in worship, a teen in unconventional dress, etc. Displaying these photos, ask, Who is made in God's image? Some of these? All of these? Suggest that the class join you in examining the Scriptures to consider what being made in God's image means.

4. Read Genesis 1:26–27 aloud. Refer members to the ideas in the lesson comments on ways we reflect God's image. That is,
   - We can think, make decisions, and accept responsibility.
   - We are by nature religious beings.
   - We are moral beings, recognizing good and evil.

   Thus, as the lesson comments state in the section on Genesis 1:26–27, "We have soul competency. God made us in the divine image, making us responsible for our decisions about relating to the Lord. No one can force true belief."

5. Ask someone to read aloud Jeremiah 31:29–34 as others follow. Ask the class to listen for thoughts that relate to soul competency. After the reading, point out that in the past, the decisions of the head of the group affected all in that group, as is seen in verse 29. Ask, Who is considered responsible according to verses 29–30?

6. Write on the board, "A New Covenant." Ask, How did the emphasis of accountability shift in verses 30–35? Who is accountable for choosing God? Can a parent choose God for a child? a child for his or her parent? a pastor for a church attendee? Can you coerce your neighbor to believe? Emphasize that others can lead, teach, and urge, but each person is accountable to God for himself or herself.

7. Invite someone to read Matthew 16:16–17 aloud. Share information from the lesson comments about the setting for these verses. Ask, According to Jesus, how did Simon Peter know that Jesus was

the Christ? Emphasize that God revealed the truth directly to Peter.

8. Ask members to read or recite aloud together John 3:16. Note that there is no elaborate hierarchy involved in receiving salvation. Again, we deal directly with God, and God deals directly with us.

9. Write on the board these two columns: The Privilege of a Priest; The Responsibility of a Priest. Ask, From what we have studied so far, what insights do you have in these areas? (List the class's responses in the columns.)

10. Point out that after reading 1 Peter 2:4–10, we may add more insights. Read the passage aloud, with members following. Use the ideas in the lesson comments to point out what likely was happening to the readers of this letter. Ask, How did the writer comfort them?

11. To find additional insights to list on the board about the privilege of a priest and the responsibility of a priest, form two groups in the class. Ask one group to concentrate on verses 5–6, and another to focus on verses 9–10. Then ask each group whether they have other ideas to list in the two columns on the board.

Encourage Application

12. Write "Priesthood of the Believer" on the board. Then cross out and add letters so that the phrase reads "Priesthood of Believers." Note that this belief applies not only to the individual, but also to individuals who have formed the church. Share insights from the last two paragraphs of the lesson comments on this topic as needed.

13. Looking at the two columns on the board, ask members to discuss how their church functions as a priesthood of believers. Are believers in your church encouraged to relate directly to God in worship, service, Bible study and interpretation, and so forth? Do we allow the "messiness" of the diversity that results? Or do we look to one group or person to speak for us to God, and for God to us?

14. Emphasize that to be a priest, we must also be a disciple—a daily follower and student of Christ. Ask the class to pray for that sort of commitment so that we may serve God well in our priesthood.

ADDITIONAL TEACHING IDEAS

Connect with Life: *Case Study.* Share this case study and ask for responses: Jan's pastor has urged her and others to vote a certain way in an upcoming election. In fact, he says he feels led by God to speak out for and against certain candidates and issues. To what extent should Jan follow her pastor's advice? On what should she base her decision?

Guide the Study: *Scripture Searching.* Review Matthew 27:50–51 and Ephesians 2:18. Ask, How do these Scriptures about the crucifixion and access to God relate to one another? Note especially that the veil's being torn from top to bottom in the temple suggests God's action in inviting us into his immediate presence.

Encourage Application: *Sermon Quotations.* Print out the following bulleted quotes on a handout. Have members read the quotes from a 1920 sermon by George W. Truett, delivered on the steps of the U.S. Capitol. Consider whether the quotes are still relevant:

- "Every one must give account of himself to God. There can be no sponsors or deputies or proxies in such a vital matter. Each one must repent for himself and believe for himself, and be baptized for himself, and answer to God for himself, both in time and eternity."
- "Let the state and the church, let the institution, however dear, and the person however near, stand aside, and let the individual soul make its own direct and immediate response to God. . . . The undelegated sovereignty of Christ makes it forever impossible for His saving grace to be manipulated by any system of human mediation whatsoever."
- "Out of these two fundamental principles, the supreme authority of the Scriptures and the right of private judgment, have come all the

historic protests . . . against unscriptural creeds, polity and rites, and against the . . . assumption of religious authority over men's consciences, whether by church or by state. Baptists regard as an enormity any attempt to force the conscience, or to constrain men, by outward penalties, to this or that form of religious belief."[2]

Notes

1. Paul W. Powell, Sermon, "The Priesthood of Every Believer," 1996. (Provided by the Baptist Distinctives Committee of the Baptist General Convention of Texas, Dallas, Texas.)

2. See George W. Truett's sermon, "Baptists and Religious Liberty," in *A Sourcebook for Baptist Heritage*, ed. H. Leon McBeth (Nashville: Broadman Press, 1990), 470. The full text of the sermon can also be accessed on the internet at this address: http://www.bjcpa.org/pubs/fultruet.html

Symbolic Understanding of Baptism and the Lord's Supper

BACKGROUND SCRIPTURES

Matthew 3:13–17; 26:26–30; 28:18–20; Mark 1:9–11;
14:22–26; Luke 3:21–22; 22:14–20; John 3:23;
Acts 2:41–42; 8:35–39; 16:30–33; 20:7; Romans 6:1–7;
1 Corinthians 10:16,21; 11:23–29; Colossians 2:12

FOCAL TEXTS

Mark 1:9–11; Romans 6:1–7; 1 Corinthians 11:23–29

MAIN IDEA

"Christ instituted two ceremonial ordinances and committed
them to his people for perpetual observance—baptism and the
Lord's Supper. These two ceremonies are pictorial
representations of the fundamental facts of the gospel and of
our salvation through the gospel."[1]

STUDY AIM

To describe the Scriptural view of the nature of baptism and the
Lord's Supper

QUICK READ

The two ordinances, baptism and the Lord's Supper, tie Baptists
together by reminding them of the commitments they have
made to God and to one another.

43

When I returned to America after two years in Vietnam as a Missionary Journeyman, I wept the first time I heard the national anthem, and I got a lump in my throat the first time I saw the American flag flying in the breeze. The flag and the anthem are just symbols. But what power they possess!

Symbols play vital roles in our lives. Yet sometimes we forget how symbols shape our thoughts and actions. Never underestimate the power of a symbol, whether a symbol of national identity or of Baptist identity.

Baptists believe that the ordinances of the Lord's Supper and baptism are symbolic. As we consider this lesson, let us remember that Baptist doctrines fit together. Because we believe in salvation by grace, we also believe that baptism and the Lord's Supper do not save a person. No act you or I do saves us from our sin. But baptism and communion are powerful symbols of our faith, and we should take them seriously. Each ordinance says something about our covenant with Christ and with the church.

Baptism, a Symbol of Commitment (Mark 1:9–11)

We do well to look to the life of Jesus to begin understanding this doctrine. In Mark 1:9–11, the author recorded Jesus' baptism by John, his cousin. John, already acknowledged as a prophet, baptized folks in the Jordan River when they publicly repented of their sin and renewed their covenant with God. Baptism for Jews symbolized repentance and becoming part of the community of faith (see sidebar, "The Background of Baptism"). John offered serious people the opportunity to make a public statement about their relationship with God, a relationship that already existed.

When Jesus chose to be baptized, he made an important public statement. He did not need to repent of sin, because Jesus did not sin (Hebrews 4:15). Jesus identified with our human dilemma and made a

Mark 1:9–11

[9]In those days Jesus came from Nazareth of Galilee and was baptized by John in the Jordan. [10]And just as he was coming up out of the water, he saw the heavens torn apart and the Spirit descending like a dove on him. [11]And a voice came from heaven, "You are my Son, the Beloved; with you I am well pleased."

Romans 6:1–7

[1]What then are we to say? Should we continue in sin in order that grace may abound? [2]By no means! How can we who died to sin go on living in it? [3]Do you not know that all of us who have been baptized into Christ Jesus were baptized into his death? [4]Therefore we have been buried with him by baptism into death, so that, just as Christ was raised from the dead by the glory of the Father, so we too might walk in newness of life.

[5]For if we have been united with him in a death like his, we will certainly be united with him in a resurrection like his. [6]We know that our old self was crucified with him so that the body of sin might be destroyed, and we might no longer be enslaved to sin. [7]For whoever has died is freed from sin.

1 Corinthians 11:23–29

[23]For I received from the Lord what I also handed on to you, that the Lord Jesus on the night when he was betrayed took a loaf of bread, [24]and when he had given thanks, he broke it and said, "This is my body that is for you. Do this in remembrance of me." [25]In the same way he took the cup also, after supper, saying, "This cup is the new covenant in my blood. Do this, as often as you drink it, in remembrance of me." [26]For as often as you eat this bread and drink the cup, you proclaim the Lord's death until he comes.

[27]Whoever, therefore, eats the bread or drinks the cup of the Lord in an unworthy manner will be answerable for the body and blood of the Lord. [28]Examine yourselves, and only then eat of the bread and drink of the cup. [29]For all who eat and drink without discerning the body, eat and drink judgment against themselves.

covenant with us and with God by his baptism. In Mark's account, the Holy Spirit descended on Jesus and a voice from heaven said, "You are my Son, the Beloved; with you I am well pleased" (Mark 1:11). For Jesus, baptism signified a covenant made and a relationship established between himself and humanity. He did not need salvation, but he did want to identify publicly with those committed to God.

Jesus accepted his role in the salvation process at his baptism. The voice from heaven put together parts of a psalm about the coming Messiah, the Promised One of Israel (Psalm 2:7), and the Servant (Isaiah 42:1) who would suffer and die for the salvation of the people. At his baptism, Jesus accepted the mantle of Messiah and Suffering Servant, two ideas that didn't flow together naturally within Judaism. Identifying with a sinning race and accepting his call, Jesus established the powerful nature of baptism as a symbol of commitment to God. Although not necessary for salvation, baptism became an important ritual of commitment to the way of God, and for humans, of turning from their old life to a new life with Christ.

Jews of Jesus' day believed in the symbolic nature of baptism. For the Jews, baptism was a symbol of entering the faith or of repentance and cleansing. However, at the time when Baptists began emerging from the Reformation in the 1600s, the general understanding of Christian baptism was that the act of baptism was part of salvation. A priest baptized babies to free them from the burden of original sin. Even in the Reformation traditions of Martin Luther and John Calvin, baptism remained more than symbol, and infants continued to be baptized into the church.

In the early 1600s, Baptists wrestled with who should be baptized and why. Baptists concluded that baptism symbolized a commitment to Christ already made and salvation already accepted. Thus, early Baptists baptized only adults who could make such a decision for Christ by themselves. In fact, as the new denomination grew, other Christians called the denomination "Baptist" because of Baptists' practice of adult believers' baptism and rejection of infant baptism. The process of understanding the role of baptism took decades. By 1644, however, when the

First London Confession was written by Baptists in that city, it clearly presented the symbolic nature of baptism:

> That Baptisme is an Ordinance of the new Testament given by Christ, to be dispensed onely upon persons professing faith, or that are Disciples, or taught, who upon profession of faith, ought to be baptized.[2]

Baptists today practice immersion when baptizing. At the beginning of the denomination's history, though, its leaders were not unanimous about the form of baptism. Accepting baptism as a symbol, Thomas Helwys, the pastor of the first Baptist church in England, felt okay with using affusion (flicking water from one's fingertips over the believer's head). Early Particular Baptists, those who believed Jesus died only for those "elected" to salvation, sprinkled believers. Particular Baptists adopted immersion as the correct form of baptism in the 1640s.

Immersion eventually became the standard form of baptism because the Greek verb *baptizo*, from which our word "baptize" comes, means "to immerse" (see sidebar, "The Background of Baptism"). As people who take Scripture seriously, Baptists identified immersion as the appropriate way to baptize people, because that is what the Bible says.

Death, Burial, and Resurrection (Romans 6:1–7)

Some folks think if an act is symbolic, it has no importance. Wrong! Baptism and the Lord's Supper are symbols, but they remain critically important to the identity of Baptists and of Christians generally. Paul thought they held great importance for the early Church and for all believers.

Paul wrote the Letter to the Romans to introduce himself to that church. He had not visited the congregation. He knew, though, of their work in the Imperial City, and they knew of his work in the provinces. Paul intended to ask for the Romans' help to make a missionary journey

The Background of Baptism

When the translators of the King James Version of the Bible came to the Greek verb *baptizo*, they had trouble. The verb means "to dip, to plunge, to immerse under water." Because the Church of England sprinkled as the rite of entry into the church, the scholars faced a problem—how to translate the verb. They solved the problem by not translating the word *baptizo*. The scholars simply brought the verb into the English language as *baptize*.

The biblical form of baptism parallels the form one experienced to become an adult convert to Judaism. Being immersed to become a Jew symbolized death to the old life and cleansing for the new life. To become a Jew, a person underwent several immersions over a period of time, but the early Christians adopted one immersion as sufficient.

The symbolism in Judaism carried over to Christianity—death, burial, and resurrection; cleansing from sin to a pure life. For the Hebrews and for Baptists, baptism is not magical and carries no power of its own, but it symbolizes a very important reality.

to Spain. To enlist their aid, he wrote the Letter of Romans to explain his beliefs and commitments. He included theological insights he felt critical to the Christian faith. Of all his letters, the one to the Roman church presents most fully what Paul believed and taught. To this book we turn to gain insight into Paul's position on the importance of baptism, looking particularly at Romans 6:1–7.

As discussed in the lesson on salvation by grace, Baptists believe that the process of salvation includes salvation from the punishment for sin (regeneration), current salvation from the power of sin (sanctification), and future salvation from the presence of sin (glorification). In Romans 6:1–7, Paul talked about these three facets of salvation and tied each one to baptism, not just baptism with water, but baptism into the life of Christ.

Dealing with the important topic of freedom from sin, Paul used powerful imagery to explain how a Christian relates to the salvation event and process. We as baptized believers share in Christ's death, burial, and resurrection. Paul explained how baptism symbolizes burial of our old selves with Christ's burial and our emergence into "newness of life" as we came out of the water (Romans 6:4). For Paul, the act of baptism meant our identification with Christ publicly, with the sorrow of his death, but also with the power of his resurrection. What hope Paul extended to us as he struggled to understand and communicate the meaning of the Christ-event!

Paul piled on promise after promise symbolized by baptism. We share Christ's death; we share Christ's burial; we share Christ's resurrection; we share the glory of Christ. No longer bound by sin, we live a new life, one powered by our commitment to God. But we also live this life in community with other believers. Baptism is a public event, a public commitment to the Lordship of Christ, a public identification with the community of faith. Paul taught that with this one act of baptism, the purpose and power of the Incarnation became clear to everyone viewing the baptism or participating in the act itself.

My church celebrates baptisms at the beginning of Sunday morning worship, and our ministers take turns officiating. One Sunday, when the youth minister baptized a couple of young people, she said something that struck me. I hadn't thought about the promise the church makes to the person being baptized. As Susan lowered and raised each young person, she reminded the congregation that as these new church members made promises to us about their commitment to Christ, we made a promise to them to help nurture and "grow" them in the faith. For the first time in a long time, the power of the symbol held me—death, burial, resurrection in Christ, *and* a commitment to the body of Christ.

Paul wrote to the church at Rome, not just to individuals who happened to hear the letter read at a worship service. For Baptists, the public act of baptism of believers by immersion signifies the commitment already made by the individual. It also symbolizes the covenant made by the congregation with the new member and with God. Jesus identified with us through baptism, and we identify with Jesus and one another through baptism. Just a symbol? Yes, but so much more, too.

Communion and Community (1 Corinthians 11:23–29)

I grew up in Southern Baptist churches from Hawaii to Virginia. Dad served in the Marine Corps. So I experienced many ways of celebrating communion. But almost always, the Lord's Supper got tacked onto the morning service or the evening service. I felt like the ministers said, "Oops, it's the end of the quarter, and we have to celebrate the Lord's Supper." I liked the grape juice a lot, but the crackers usually didn't taste very good. I had friends, members of other denominations, who had communion every Sunday. I decided it would be really boring to have to go through this stuff every week. Since that time, after studying the reason we celebrate the Lord's Supper, I realize that as an immature Christian, I was so very, very wrong to think of communion as boring.

Paul wrote the oldest description of the Lord's Supper in his First Letter to the Corinthian church. For the apostle, communion gave the church a specific, designated time to reflect on the price of our salvation. The Lord's Supper focused hearts and minds on what Jesus endured in order for believers to experience God's saving grace. "Do this in remembrance of me" (1 Corinthians 11:24). Each time we partake of communion, we remember Jesus' sacrifice on our behalf. Too, we have an opportunity to examine our hearts and take care of any unfinished business between ourselves and God. Only a symbol—but one that has the power to confront us with our spiritual need.

In 1 Corinthians 11:23–29, the apostle laid down the "elements" for celebrating communion—"a loaf of bread," "the cup," spiritual self-examination, and a community of faith. Interpreting the Lord's Supper as symbolic and not necessary for salvation, Baptists' celebration of communion includes these elements in one form or another. Through the years, we have argued over whether to use wine or grape juice to represent Christ's blood. We have argued over whether to use unleavened bread or broken crackers to represent Christ's broken body. Should we use individual cups? Should we make everyone come to the front to take the elements? Should we break the bread up first or let everyone take a chunk on their own? In fact, perhaps we argued so much over the details of communion that we sometimes forgot the *point* of the Lord's Supper—that Jesus' body was broken for us, that Jesus' blood was shed for us.

Self-examination is also part of communion. Have you ever refused to participate in the Lord's Supper because of your spiritual condition? Do we think about the current state of our soul as we pass the bread and juice? Now and then, something forces me to assess my spiritual condition during communion. When I do, the time of worship becomes more meaningful. This symbol of Christ's sacrifice highlights the petty nature of most of my spiritual complaints. This symbol blows away the smoke I wrap around my sin to hide it from God. This symbol provides me with the time to respond anew to God's grace with repentance for my current spiritual failures.

Paul came down hard on people who breezed by the self-examination part of communion. In verse 29, he wrote that folks who blithely take the Lord's Supper with no thought for their own relationship with God "eat and drink judgment against themselves." I have no idea what that means in eternal terms, but it sounds bad! In my own life, I know that when I ignore the need to "get right with God," I suffer a sense of separation I don't like. Should we take more seriously Paul's command to examine ourselves, and "only then eat of the bread and drink of the cup" (11:28). Food for thought.

Historically, Baptists recognize communion as an activity of the body of Christ, the community of faith. Jesus shared the bread and the cup in the upper room with the community of the Twelve. We share the bread and cup with our community of faith. If your church has a ministry that takes the Lord's Supper to homebound members, why do you do this? You do it to strengthen the homebound person's sense of "oneness" with the congregation by sharing communion. I suppose it's possible for one person to celebrate the Lord's Supper and find it meaningful, but the presence of like-minded sisters and brothers in Christ makes the celebration much more powerful. Whether grape juice or wine, whether bread or crackers, the symbol of communion gains strength when shared within the body of Christ.

Some Baptists disagree about who should participate in the celebration of communion in the local church. Some folks think anyone confessing Christ as Lord qualifies for the celebration. Others think only Baptists should participate in the Lord's Supper. Still others include only members of that local Baptist church in the celebration. Historically, Baptists were all over the map on this issue. English Baptists argued in the 1700s over whether they should include John Bunyan's church in their fellowship, because he served communion to any Christian. In America, the Landmark movement leaders of the 1800s protested that only local church members should take communion.

According to Baptist doctrine, each congregation must decide whom to include and whom to exclude when celebrating the Lord's Supper. I would suppose, however, that when we get to heaven, God will have no

Case Study

You have a good Christian friend visiting from out of town. This friend goes to church with you on the Sunday that your congregation celebrates the Lord's Supper. Your friend is a Methodist and wants to participate in the Lord's Supper. What do you tell your friend? What do *you* think about the issue?

restrictions on which of the residents of heaven can come to the heavenly table.

Taking the Symbols Seriously

Baptism and the Lord's Supper are two powerful symbols of our individual and corporate relationship with God. All of us need to take these celebrations more seriously and more thoughtfully. As Baptists we affirm their importance. As Baptists, let us take our own affirmation to heart and take these two ordinances more seriously.

QUESTIONS

1. What is most meaningful to you about baptism?

2. What is most meaningful to you about the Lord's Supper?

3. What might your church do to enhance the meaningfulness of the celebration of the two ordinances?

4. Do you feel uncomfortable when attending another church that does communion or baptism differently? Why?

Notes

1. Walter Thomas Conner, *Christian Doctrine* (Nashville, Tennessee: Broadman Press, 1937), 273.
2. William L. Lumpkin, *Baptist Confessions of Faith*, rev. ed. (Valley Forge: Judson Press, 1969), 167.

Symbolic Understanding of Baptism and the Lord's Supper

TEACHING AIM

To lead participants to describe the Scriptural view of the nature of baptism and the Lord's Supper

TEACHING PLAN

Connect with Life

1. Ask, Have you (or anyone you know) ever lost a wedding ring? How did you feel? Why? Point out that a ring is only a symbol of the marriage; it is not nearly so important as the marriage itself. Having said that, symbols are important! A wedding ring says to the world that you have committed yourself to another person, above everyone else. Thus people search diligently when they lose a symbol of something so precious. They prize that symbol.

2. Suggest that today we will look at two symbols Baptists value because they remind us of our commitments to Christ. They are two ceremonial ordinances that Christ himself instituted—baptism and the Lord's Supper.

Guide the Study

3. Ask someone to read aloud Mark 1:9–11 about Jesus' baptism and to consider what Jesus' baptism meant. After receiving responses, note that Jesus did not need to repent and be saved, but in this act he publicly identified with those committed to God. It was a symbol of commitment to God. Even today, baptism does not save us. Rather, baptism testifies to our commitment to God.

4. Ask members to review silently the lesson comments on the history of baptism, which are found in the last three paragraphs under the heading, "Baptism, a Symbol of Commitment (Mark 1:9–11)." The section to be reviewed begins with "In the early 1600s . . ." and ends with ". . . what the Bible says." Ask the class to be prepared to finish this sentence: One thing I learned from this history is . . . .

5. Refer to the next passage of Scripture, Romans 6:1–7, and summarize the lesson comments about the background of Romans. Note that Paul's Letter to the Romans gives us important theological insights into baptism's importance to Christians. Ask a member to read aloud Romans 6:1–7, with others following and listening for how baptism symbolizes the experience of salvation.

6. After the reading, point out that for Paul, baptism meant that we identified with Christ in
   • His death
   • His power
   • His promise
   Write these bulleted phrases on the board, and ask members to identify phrases from verses 3–7 that show these ideas. Consider these possible answers: His death (buried with him, "united with him in a death like his," "crucified with him"); His power (raised, "united with him in a resurrection like his"); His promise ("walk in newness of life," "united with him in a resurrection like his")

7. Also in relation to these three areas, ask: According to these verses, how do we die to sin? How do we walk "in newness of life"? What does God promise us?

8. Summarize these beliefs about baptism the class has explored:
   a. We are saved not by baptism, but by grace.
   b. Baptism is for believers only.
   c. Baptists immerse because of the biblical example. (To reinforce this idea, refer to the sidebar, "The Background of Baptism.")
   d. Baptism symbolizes to the world the death, burial, and resurrection of Christ—and our relationship with him.

9. Note the prominent location of the baptistry in Baptist church buildings. Also note that Baptists have found rivers, pools, and other places to baptize. Ask, How do these practices suggest the importance of the symbol?

10. Now invite the class to read about another important celebration for Christians, the Lord's Supper, in 1 Corinthians 11:23–29. Invite someone to read the passage aloud, and encourage the class to listen for ideas about the meaning of the Lord's Supper.

11. Note that believers have used wine and grape juice; loaves, crackers, and unleavened bread—all as "elements" for celebrating the Supper. But the main point is what these physical things symbolize. Ask what that is, according to Scripture (see 11:26, "the Lord's death").

12. Note that taking the bread and the cup is only a part of the Lord's Supper. According to verses 27–29, this must also be a serious exercise in self-examination. If we examine our hearts and renew our commitment to Christ during this ceremony, our practical day-to-day lives will be changed—in remembrance of Christ!

13. Write "communion" on the board. Ask, Why is the Lord's Supper often referred to as "communion"? Suggest that the Lord's Supper is shared in the presence of the Lord and one's fellow believers. Note that both baptism and the Lord's Supper are observed in the

presence of others. The two observances strengthen the body of Christ and give participants the opportunity to proclaim their identification with Christ.

Encourage Application

14. Ask members to consider the past, present, and future when next celebrating the Lord's Supper:
    • The past—What did Christ's death do for me?
    • The present—What is my present spiritual condition?
    • The future—I'll "proclaim the Lord's death until he comes" (11:26).
15. Ask the class to consider how we can maintain the personal meaningfulness of every baptism we observe and every Lord's Supper in which we participate. For example, how might we personally prepare for these experiences? What can our local church do to make them more meaningful?

ADDITIONAL TEACHING IDEAS

Connect with Life: *Symbols.* Ask class members what their country's flag means to them. Note that although the flag in itself is not freedom or our country, it is still deeply important and should thus be respected as a symbol. This same idea is true of the serious symbolism of baptism and the Lord's Supper. As the Scriptures reveal, they are not our salvation, but they symbolize our relationship with Christ. Thus we are to take them seriously.

Guide the Study: *What the Ordinances Teach.* George W. Truett called baptism and the Lord's Supper "teaching ordinances."[1] As you study the Scriptures for this lesson, list on the board what each ordinance teaches us. In other words, what does it show us about Christ, about ourselves, and about our lives in Christ?

Encourage Application: *Discussion Question.* Point out that Baptists have insisted that a person be converted before baptism and that often in the past, a person had to give an oral testimony to the church before being accepted for baptism. Baptist historian William Estep adds: "Since it is faith in Christ and not baptism that saves, it is far better to delay baptism when the validity of a profession of faith is in doubt than to baptize prematurely."[2] Do you agree or disagree?

Encourage Application: *Case Study.* Refer to and discuss the case study about the Lord's Supper in the sidebar in the lesson comments.

Notes

1. See George W. Truett's sermon, "Baptists and Religious Liberty," in *A Sourcebook for Baptist Heritage*, ed. H. Leon McBeth (Nashville: Broadman Press, 1990), 470. The full text of the sermon can also be accessed on the internet at this address: http://www.bjcpa.org/pubs/fultruet.html
2. William R. Estep, *Why Baptists? A Study of Baptist Faith and Heritage* (Dallas: BAPTISTWAY, 1997).

The Autonomy of the Local Congregation of Believers

BACKGROUND SCRIPTURES

Matthew 18:15–20; Acts 6:3–6; 13:1–3; 14:23,27; 15:1–30; 16:5; 20:28; 1 Corinthians 1:2; 5:1–5; Revelation 2—3

FOCAL TEXTS

Matthew 18:15–20; Acts 6:3–6; 13:1–3; 1 Corinthians 5:1–5

MAIN IDEA

"Each local church is self-governing and independent in the management of its affairs."[1]

STUDY AIM

To explain why Baptists believe that each local church is autonomous and identify implications of this idea

QUICK READ

Members of a local Baptist church have the responsibility and privilege of making the decisions that chart the church's course. No external authority can tell a Baptist church what to do.

When the controversy in the Southern Baptist Convention erupted at the 1979 Houston meeting, confused reporters needed lots of help. They didn't understand how decisions made in Houston held no power over the local church to make changes. Glenn Hilburn, a friend of mine and a professor of church history at Baylor University, held briefings to explain the structure of Baptist churches, associations, and the national organization to the non-Baptist reporters. The media representatives still shook their heads and murmured. They couldn't comprehend a people whose national organization did not dictate the actions of the local church. Sometimes I'll have a non-Baptist in my Baptist History class, and they, like the reporters, struggle with how Baptists operate.

Baptists structure their churches as congregations in which the members make the decisions and choose to cooperate with other like-minded churches. This polity (structure) makes sense when you look at the Baptist doctrines we've studied. Salvation by grace, soul competency, priesthood of the believers, symbolic ordinances—it makes sense that Baptist church structure reflects the basic belief in the individual responsibility of a believer to work for the kingdom of God, share the gospel, and join a community of faith for nurture and growth. Of course the individual believer would have a voice in the governance of the church! We call this way of doing a church's work the autonomy of the local church. "Autonomy" comes from the Greek words *autos* and *nomos*, meaning "self" and "law." An autonomous church rules itself.

Many Christian denominations structure their churches and the relationships between congregations differently than Baptists do. Each type of church structure rests on a certain interpretation of biblical passages. When Baptists developed in the early 1600s and searched Scripture for their model of church polity, they understood the overall sense of Scripture to support a congregational model as we have today. Acts 6:3–6 taught them that churches choose their own leaders. Matthew 18:15–20 and 1 Corinthians 5:1–5 taught them that churches decide how to discipline members. And Acts 13:1–3 taught them that local churches choose people for ministry as led by the Holy Spirit.

Matthew 18:15-20

[15]"If another member of the church sins against you, go and point out the fault when the two of you are alone. If the member listens to you, you have regained that one. [16]But if you are not listened to, take one or two others along with you, so that every word may be confirmed by the evidence of two or three witnesses. [17]If the member refuses to listen to them, tell it to the church; and if the offender refuses to listen even to the church, let such a one be to you as a Gentile and a tax collector. [18]Truly I tell you, whatever you bind on earth will be bound in heaven, and whatever you loose on earth will be loosed in heaven. [19]Again, truly I tell you, if two of you agree on earth about anything you ask, it will be done for you by my Father in heaven. [20]For where two or three are gathered in my name, I am there among them."

Acts 6:3-6

[3]Therefore, friends, select from among yourselves seven men of good standing, full of the Spirit and of wisdom, whom we may appoint to this task, [4]while we, for our part, will devote ourselves to prayer and to serving the word." [5]What they said pleased the whole community, and they chose Stephen, a man full of faith and the Holy Spirit, together with Philip, Prochorus, Nicanor, Timon, Parmenas, and Nicolaus, a proselyte of Antioch. [6]They had these men stand before the apostles, who prayed and laid their hands on them.

Acts 13:1-3

[1]Now in the church at Antioch there were prophets and teachers: Barnabas, Simeon who was called Niger, Lucius of Cyrene, Manaen a member of the court of Herod the ruler, and Saul. [2]While they were worshiping the Lord and fasting, the Holy Spirit said, "Set apart for me Barnabas and Saul for the work to which I have called them." [3]Then after fasting and praying they laid their hands on them and sent them off.

1 Corinthians 5:1-5

¹It is actually reported that there is sexual immorality among you, and of a kind that is not found even among pagans; for a man is living with his father's wife. ²And you are arrogant! Should you not rather have mourned, so that he who has done this would have been removed from among you?

³For though absent in body, I am present in spirit; and as if present I have already pronounced judgment ⁴in the name of the Lord Jesus on the man who has done such a thing. When you are assembled, and my spirit is present with the power of our Lord Jesus, ⁵you are to hand this man over to Satan for the destruction of the flesh, so that his spirit may be saved in the day of the Lord.

God Is Present . . . (Acts 6:3-6)

God is present where two or three are gathered in the Lord's name (Matthew 18:20). So, wherever believers gather, they have the leadership of the Holy Spirit as a community of faith. They thus can make all the decisions necessary as a congregation. As individuals, each person carries the responsibility to live for God, to interpret Scripture, and to be Christ in the world. But as a community of faith, God's presence sharpens those responsibilities and focuses them for the good of the church.

In Acts 6:3–6, God focused the concept of service for the Jerusalem church. The apostles spent their time in worship and teaching the new Christians. They didn't have time to take care of the needy of the congregation. Under Jewish law, God required believers to take special care of widows and orphans. The Greek-speaking widows in the Jerusalem church felt neglected by the leaders. The church solved the problem by choosing from the congregation seven people to act as servants in distributing food and other necessities to the needy. For our study this week, the important point is that the people chose the servants. Peter and the other apostles did not say, "You, you, and you." Rather, they relied on the Holy Spirit working in the average church member to choose wisely.

The folks in the congregation looked for Spirit-filled and God-directed believers who could do the job. The members worked from their knowledge of each other and what the job required. Once the congregation chose the seven servants, the apostles set the men aside for special duties in a public ceremony. The public ceremony did not give the men special power. The laying on of hands simply indicated to the assembly that the servants accepted their new responsibilities and that the church made a covenant with them to help with the work. The members of the congregation chose wisely, for the servants did the job and did it well.

In Acts 6:3–6, the autonomy of the local church shines through. People perceived a need. The congregation, under the leadership of the Holy Spirit, determined a way to meet the need. The members chose people to do the actual work. No one told the congregation what they must do. No one ordered the selection of certain people. No one said, "If you don't do it this way, you aren't a true believer."

For Baptists, the Bible affirms that the local church is responsible for its own business, both spiritual and practical. The congregation may choose to cooperate with others, as in an association or convention, but "other groups or churches cannot take away the decision-making responsibilities of the local congregation."[2] God is present where two or three are gathered, and those two or three must make their own decisions under God's leadership.

When Decisions Have to Be Made . . .
(Matthew 18:15–20; 1 Corinthians 5:1–5)

When I teach Church History or Baptist History and come to the lecture on church discipline, the topic always creates discomfort. No one wants to be seen as judgmental or fanatical. Saying to fellow church members that they need to mend their ways requires special care. Thankfully, this lesson centers on the autonomy of the local church. So I don't have to deal specifically with the issue of church discipline. But we will focus on these passages as they make the point that the local church, and not some external agency or group, chooses what shall and shall not require discipline.

The New Testament teaches that the local church has responsibility for taking care of both practical and spiritual matters in its midst. Both Matthew 18:15–20 and 1 Corinthians 5:1–5 clearly note that the local folks must make decisions for the good of the congregation as well as the good of individual members. In some denominations, discipline is ordered by a hierarchy outside the local church. For Baptists, discipline remains within the control of the local congregation. Furthermore, discipline is a congregational decision, not the decision of one or two people.

These passages assert that God's presence with a group of believers establishes the necessary power for making decisions. Matthew 18 does not say you must wait until an outside authority gives an order before your congregation can act. In 1 Corinthians 5, Paul urged the community of faith to remove an immoral member. Paul, however, also recognized that the action must result from the leadership of God. Central to Baptist thought lies the notion that the corporate consciousness of Christ comes through when a congregation meets to make a decision. Paul's concerns, aired in a meeting and commented on, might galvanize the Corinthian church to take action. Still, Paul could only suggest action. The final decision rested with the folks in Corinth and how they perceived God's leadership.

From the days of the New Testament, local churches have cooperated with one another to accomplish greater good. In Romans 16:1–2, we learn that churches accepted members from other congregations. First Corinthians 16:1–4 shows that churches pooled their resources in a good cause. And the existence of the New Testament itself proves that churches shared letters and information among themselves for the good of all (Colossians 4:16–17).[3] While acting as autonomous churches, congregations still cooperated in many endeavors.

For modern Baptists, the issue becomes complicated because autonomous local churches have chosen to relate to one another and cooperate to accomplish tasks that single congregations could not. We relate to other Baptist churches in our geographical area through the local association and the state convention. Each group we relate to has the right and responsibility to set standards for the relationship. We as a church have a voice in establishing those standards. If for some reason we deviate from the standards set, then the association or convention has the authority to "dis-fellowship" us, to withdraw cooperation, and we must go on our way. Each level of relationship makes its own decisions based on what the members believe to be right.

For example, one Baptist association chose to welcome a woman as pastor of one of the churches. Affirming the local congregation members' right to choose their own pastor, the association treated and worked with her church as it had for decades. Another association nearby chose to "dis-fellowship" a church for calling a woman minister. For the members of that association, the standard of who could be a church minister did

Setting People Apart for Service

In the New Testament, a church would set people apart in public ceremonies for special tasks, as with the Antioch congregation laying hands on Paul and Barnabas (Acts 13:1–3). Such a ceremony was not a requirement to be met before becoming a minister. The Bible emphasizes that the lives of the people chosen for special work, whether Phoebe of Cenchreae (Romans 16:1), Philip of Samaria (Acts 6:5), or Epaphroditus of Philippi (Philippians 2:25), bore testimony to God's presence. The Holy Spirit led and reinforced the congregation's decision.

not include women. Thus that association excluded the congregation in question. For our purposes in this lesson, I must affirm both decisions. Both decisions recognized that the local church must make its own choices, but also that those choices carry consequences. However I feel personally about the "right" or "wrong" of women in ministry—and as a woman minister in the teaching profession, I have strong opinions!—both associations acted within mainstream Baptist doctrine because neither dictated to the local church who must be their pastor.

Baptists historically have affirmed local church autonomy, but we also have asserted cooperation for missions, evangelism, and so forth. Many churches working together accomplish more than one church. In 1814 churches across America joined together to support Anne Hazeltine and Adoniram Judson as missionaries by forming the Baptist General Missionary Convention. When these churches joined together, they agreed to work together for missions. Note that as individual churches they differed greatly! They worshiped in different ways. They had different concepts of who should be church leaders. They felt differently about including people of other races in their memberships. They had different concepts of the atonement and the work of the Holy Spirit. However, they all agreed that God wanted them to support and do missions. So they put aside their differences, differences they saw as less important than missions. They focused on the all-important task of missions.

Your Spiritual Gifts

Knowing your spiritual gifts will help you decide in which areas of church service to engage. Determine your gifts by talking with Christian friends who know you well, thinking about what you like to do and do well in the church, and praying for God to show you what gifts the Spirit has placed in your life. Read 1 Corinthians 12:4–11 and Ephesians 4:11–13 to see whether one or more of those gifts fits you.

Mainstream Baptists have worked to accept diversity while maintaining cooperation among congregations. In 1845, the Southern Baptist Convention split from the General Missionary Convention because the difference in the Northern and Southern views of slavery caused too much trouble.

In recent years, splits have occurred among Baptists because a church's concept of Scripture or of ministry or of missions or of ministerial authority differed too much from what a group accepted as true. A tough question facing twenty-first-century Baptists is, "How much difference is too much?" In the past, Baptists have accepted a great deal of difference and still cooperated. Today, mainstream Baptists still accept differences and cooperate. How much difference is "too much"? And who answers that question for you?

Concerning the Work of the Kingdom . . . (Acts 13:1–3)

I grew up attending Sunbeams, GAs, and YWAs. I served as a Journeyman missionary. Missions was, is, and always will be important to me. So, with great pleasure, I turn our attention to the concept of local church autonomy as it worked out in missions in the first century.

The story should be familiar to you. Barnabas, the Son of Encouragement, traveled to Antioch of Syria because the Jerusalem church heard that a Christian congregation had taken root there and was growing rapidly. Barnabas found the young congregation thriving and on target with their understanding of the gospel. Calling in Paul to help teach and nurture the young believers, the two men worked with the church for more than a year (Acts 11:19–30).

As the congregation was worshiping and fasting, the Holy Spirit led the congregation to "set apart" these two leaders "for the work to which I have called them" (13:2). In Judaism and early Christianity, a person fasted to emphasize the importance of a serious request. A person also fasted to focus on prayer and the will of God. So, because the people in Antioch wanted to know God's will, and they were serious about the effort, the Holy Spirit led the congregation to set aside Barnabas and Paul for special work. The Antioch folks became the first missionary sending organization! And Paul and Barnabas, the first full-fledged missionaries!

The local church made the choice under God's leadership. The local congregation responded to the prompting of the Holy Spirit in choosing the ones to be sent. The local church thus is seen to be the basic organizational building block of Baptist missionary efforts.

Over the years, the way churches did missions changed. In 1792, British Baptists formed the Baptist Missionary Society to send William and Dorothy Carey, and others, to India to preach the gospel. In 1814, the General Missionary Convention was formed in America to support Anne Hazeltine and Adoniram Judson's work in Burma. In 1845, when Southern Baptists split from the General Convention, the messengers to the formation convention established the Foreign Mission Board and the Domestic Mission Board before anything else. Why the move away from the Antioch model of an individual church sending missionaries?

The basic answer is that Baptists are a practical people. They figured out that by pooling funds, they could send more missionaries, and equip them better, than a single church could. Because missions carried such importance, most Baptist churches modified their concern for absolute local autonomy to participate in the larger missions effort. However, some folks did not believe the Bible authorized any agency beyond the local church. Thus they refused to be part of missionary societies or conventions. These congregations, known as Anti-Mission Baptists, acted true to their Baptist heritage of local church decision-making. They chose not to join associations or conventions. If one of these churches engaged in missions or evangelism, it pursued the activity without help from others.

For the Anti-Mission Baptists, the cooperating Baptists moved too far from a certain interpretation of Scripture, and so fellowship was broken. For the cooperating Baptists, the Anti-Mission folks interpreted the Bible too narrowly. The command to preach the gospel to the world held more importance than an interpretation condemning missionary organizations beyond the local church. Both groups took seriously the autonomy of the local church, but they understood that autonomy differently when they related it to the Great Commission.

A Current Concern

A modern development threatening the Baptist doctrine of the autonomy of the local church is the adoption by some congregations of the business model with a CEO running the operation. If the pastor functions as a CEO, and the paid ministerial staff work for the pastor, what role does the congregational member have? When the CEO makes all the decisions and simply informs the congregation, what remains for the member to do besides supply money? This increasingly popular organizational model is not Baptist, and it undercuts the rights and privileges of individual members of the congregation. Ministers, in Baptist life, are not "rulers." They are "servants." Remember, ultimately we are all priests.

QUESTIONS

1. What do you think of the CEO model for a pastor? Why might folks prefer that model to the historical Baptist model?

2. How seriously do you take your responsibilities as a church member?

3. Whose responsibility is the running of the church? the mission of the church? the finances of the church?

Notes

1. Walter Thomas Conner, *Christian Doctrine* (Nashville, Tennessee: Broadman Press, 1937), 266.
2. Rosalie Beck, "The Church is Free to Make Its Own Decisions under the Lordship of Christ," in *Defining Baptist Convictions for the Twenty-First Century*, ed. Charles W. Deweese (Franklin, Tennessee: Providence House Publishers, 1996), 131.
3. H. Leon McBeth, "Autonomy and Cooperation," in the *Foundations of Baptist Heritage Series* (Nashville, Tennessee: The Historical Commission of the Southern Baptist Convention, 1989), 1.

The Autonomy of the Local Congregation of Believers

TEACHING AIM

To help participants explain why Baptists believe that each local church is autonomous and identify implications of this idea

TEACHING PLAN

Connect with Life

1. Remind members that the previous lesson was about baptism and the Lord's Supper. Throughout Baptist history, Baptists have had disagreements as to the particulars of these ordinances, such as: After a person is saved, should there be other requirements met (classes, a public testimony, etc.) before he or she is baptized? As to the Lord's Supper, should any Christian be able to participate, or only members of the local congregation? Ask members to decide the correct answer to *who* decides these issues: (a) the Southern Baptist Convention; (b) the state convention; (c) the local association of churches; or (d) the local congregation. If members answer *d*, they already know something about the autonomy of the local church!

2. Share this story: When Dr. Bill Pinson was Executive Director of the Baptist General Convention of Texas, a government official

asked him to "go and straighten out" a Baptist church that was not following the law. Dr. Pinson replied: "There is no Baptist or Baptist group who has authority over a church, who [can] 'straighten them out.'" When the official then demanded to speak "to the person . . . in charge of Baptists," Dr. Pinson suggested that only by prayer could he do that "because Jesus Christ was the only One 'in charge' of a Baptist church.'"[1]

Guide the Study

3. Note that whenever a group—however small or large—gathers in the name of Christ, Christ has made a promise to them. Read this promise together in Matthew 18:20.

4. Point out that Jesus made this beautiful promise in Matthew 18:20 as he instructed his disciples on the thorny issue of disciplining a fellow believer. Invite someone to read aloud Jesus' words in Matthew 18:15–20, and encourage the class to listen for what this passage suggests about decision-making in the church. Ask members to comment on who had authority in this example.
   • An individual? To what extent?
   • Several people? To what extent?
   • The believer's church? To what extent?
   • God? To what extent?

5. Suggest that although some particulars in the application of biblical discipline may be open to interpretation, two ideas seem clear:
   • God has ultimate authority over the church.
   • No outside person or group of people disciplines the member. Rather, the local congregation does so.

6. Ask someone to read aloud 1 Corinthians 5:1–5, about another example of the church's need to discipline members who were immoral. Note that here Paul's advice was very direct, and yet he acknowledged the spirit of Christ within the local assembly. Ultimately the action

must be theirs. (If in reading this passage, your class members disagree as to *how much* authority Paul had in removing the immoral man, you may wish to point out that independence in interpretation is part of what makes us Baptists!)

7. Ask, What significance do you see in the fact that Paul wrote most of his letters to churches, not just to church leaders? Do you see a connection between the belief we studied earlier—the priesthood of the believer—and the autonomy of the local congregation?

8. Write these words on the board or on a poster you prepare ahead of time:
   - The dilemma—What was the need? (Acts 6:1–2)
   - The decision—Who decided on the seven? (6:3–5)
   - The delegation—Who decided on the men best suited for this ministry? (6:5–6)

   Divide the class into three groups, each answering a question. (If you prefer not to form groups, you could do this activity with the whole class.)

9. Ask, Have you ever noticed how God's Word is so practical? Ask members to read the following statements to see whether they apply to your local church. (You will need to print them out beforehand.)
   a. "The local church is accessible, meeting where members live."
   b. "It meets frequently, providing opportunity for participation and spiritual nurture."
   c. "It offers possibility for a diversity which is not afforded by small groups."
   d. "It is more personal and flexible than general bodies such as state and national gatherings."[2]
   e. "Included in the process [of determining God's guidance] are careful Bible study, deliberation, and prayer . . . followed by a vote of the congregation to determine the will of the majority. . . . It is still the best way for a congregation to seek God's leadership in matters not specifically dealt with in scripture."[3]

10. For another biblical example of the local church at work, ask members to read Acts 13:1–3. Ask, How serious was this church about following the Lord? What actions in these verses tell us that?

11. With the class, look especially at verse 2. Ask, Who told the church at Antioch to send Barnabas and Saul as missionaries?

12. Note that our Baptist ancestors feared that a "denominational organization . . . would try to exercise authority over churches, telling them what to believe and how to function." However, in time, "they realized that through voluntary cooperation—a 'fellowship in the gospel' (Philippians 1:5)—no autonomy would be lost but much could be gained in effectiveness for evangelism, missions, and ministry."[4] Ask, Is the idea of moving beyond the Antioch model in order to evangelize and minister cooperatively a good idea today?

Encourage Application

13. Ask, Whose responsibility is it to call a pastor? determine the church's budget? make decisions as to who can serve as clergy, deacons, and teachers? be involved in missions? Give each person a card that reads "The buck stops here." Note that under the Holy Spirit's guidance, we should not slip into the attitude of "They ought to do thus and so." We *are* the "they"!

ADDITIONAL TEACHING IDEAS

Connect with Life or Make Application: *Poster and Quiz.* Write on a poster, handout, or overhead beforehand:

- *Episcopal System*—Authority is exercised by a hierarchy beginning with bishops, then priests or pastors, then local church members.
- *Presbyterian System*—Authority is held by a body of elders, which includes both clergy and laypersons, in each local church. Authority

outside the local church is drawn from these bodies of elders.

• *Congregational System*—Authority rests in members of the local congregation. The local church may relate to larger denominational bodies, but no denominational body has authority over the local church.

Give this brief quiz orally. The correct answers are in brackets.

a. Which system finds some precedent in the New Testament? (All three!)

b. Which modern denominations are "episcopal" in government? (Included are Roman Catholic, Eastern Orthodox, Anglican, Episcopal, Methodist, with different variations.)

c. Which denominations are "presbyterian"? (Included are Presbyterian, Reformed.)

d. Which denominations are "congregational"? (Included are Congregationalists, Disciples of Christ, Churches of Christ, Baptists.)

e. Which govern from the top down? (The first two.)

f. Which govern from the bottom up? (The third one.)

g. Why have Baptists chosen to be congregational? (Because we believe in the Holy Spirit's calling and gifting each Christian—the priesthood of the believer—and consider congregational church government to be the extension of that belief.)

Notes

1. William M. Pinson, Jr., Sermon, "The Baptist Way," 1996. (Provided by the Baptist Distinctives Committee of the Baptist General Convention of Texas, Dallas, Texas.)
2. W. Boyd Hunt, *Redeemed! Eschatological Redemption and the Kingdom of God* (Nashville: Broadman, 1993), 219–220.
3. Hunt, *Redeemed*, 223.
4. Pinson, "The Baptist Way."

Beliefs Important to Baptists

Here's how to order more copies of this issue and the other Bible study units in the series, *Beliefs Important to Baptists*. The *Teacher's Edition* contains teaching suggestions plus the lesson comments that appear in the member's edition. *Beliefs Important to Baptists: I, II, and III* each contain four lessons.

Please fill in the following information:

TITLE OF ITEM	PRICE	QUANTITY	COST
Who in the World Are Baptists, Anyway?	$ .45	_____	_____
Who in the World Are Baptists, Anyway?— TEACHER'S EDITION	$ .55	_____	_____
Beliefs Important to Baptists: I • The Authority of the Bible • Believer's Baptism and Church Membership • Congregational Church Government • Evangelism and Missions	$1.35	_____	_____
Beliefs Important to Baptists: I— TEACHER'S EDITION	$1.75	_____	_____
Beliefs Important to Baptists: II • Salvation Only by Grace Through Faith • Soul Competency and the Priesthood of the Believer • Baptism and the Lord's Supper • The Autonomy of the Local Congregation	$1.35	_____	_____
Beliefs Important to Baptists: II— TEACHER'S EDITION	$1.75	_____	_____
Beliefs Important to Baptists: III • The Deity and Lordship of Jesus Christ • The Security of the Believer • Voluntary Cooperation Among Churches • Religious Freedom and Separation of Church and State	$1.35	_____	_____
Beliefs Important to Baptists: III— TEACHER'S EDITION	$1.75	_____	_____

Subtotal   _____

Shipping*   _____

TOTAL   _____

*Charges for standard shipping service:
Subtotal up to $20.00 $3.95
Subtotal $20.01—$50.00 $4.95
Subtotal $50.01—$100.00   10% of subtotal
Subtotal $100.01 and up   8% of subtotal

Please allow three weeks for standard delivery. For express shipping service:
Call 1-800-355-5285 for information on additional charges.

Your name _____

Your church _____

Mailing address _____

_____

City _____ State _____ Zip _____

MAIL this form with your check
for the total amount to
Bible Study/Discipleship Division
Baptist General Convention of Texas
333 North Washington
Dallas, TX 75246-1798
(Make checks to "Baptist General Convention of Texas.")

OR, **FAX** your order anytime to:
214-828-5187, and we will bill you.

OR, **CALL** your order toll-free: 1-800-355-5285
(8:30 a.m.-5:00 p.m., M-F), and we will bill you.

OR, **E-MAIL** your order to our internet e-mail address:
baptistway@bgct.org, and we will bill you.

We look forward to receiving your order! Thank you!